STING
IF ON A WINTER'S NIGHT...

WISE PUBLICATIONS
part of The Music Sales Group
London/New York/Paris/Sydney/Copenhagen/Berlin/Tokyo/Madrid

Published by
Wise Publications
14-15 Berners Street, London W1T 3LJ, UK.

Exclusive Distributors:
Music Sales Limited
Distribution Centre, Newmarket Road,
Bury St Edmunds, Suffolk IP33 3YB, UK.

Music Sales Pty Limited
20 Resolution Drive, Caringbah,
NSW 2229, Australia.

Order No. AM999262
ISBN 978-1-84938-355-4

This book © Copyright 2009 Wise Publications,
a division of Music Sales Limited.

Unauthorised reproduction of any part of this
publication by any means including photocopying
is an infringement of copyright.

Edited by Jenni Wheeler.
Music arranged by Vasco Hexel.

www.musicsales.com

Printed in the EU.

1 Gabriel's Message... 6
2 Soul Cake... 10
3 There Is No Rose of Such Virtue... 18
4 The Snow It Melts the Soonest... 25
5 Christmas at Sea... 29
6 Lo, How a Rose E'er Blooming... 38
7 Cold Song... 42
8 The Burning Babe... 46
9 Now Winter Comes Slowly... 51
10 The Hounds of Winter... 54
11 Balulalow... 61
12 Cherry Tree Carol... 66
13 Lullaby for an Anxious Child... 68
14 Hurdy-Gurdy Man... 73
15 You Only Cross My Mind in Winter... 77

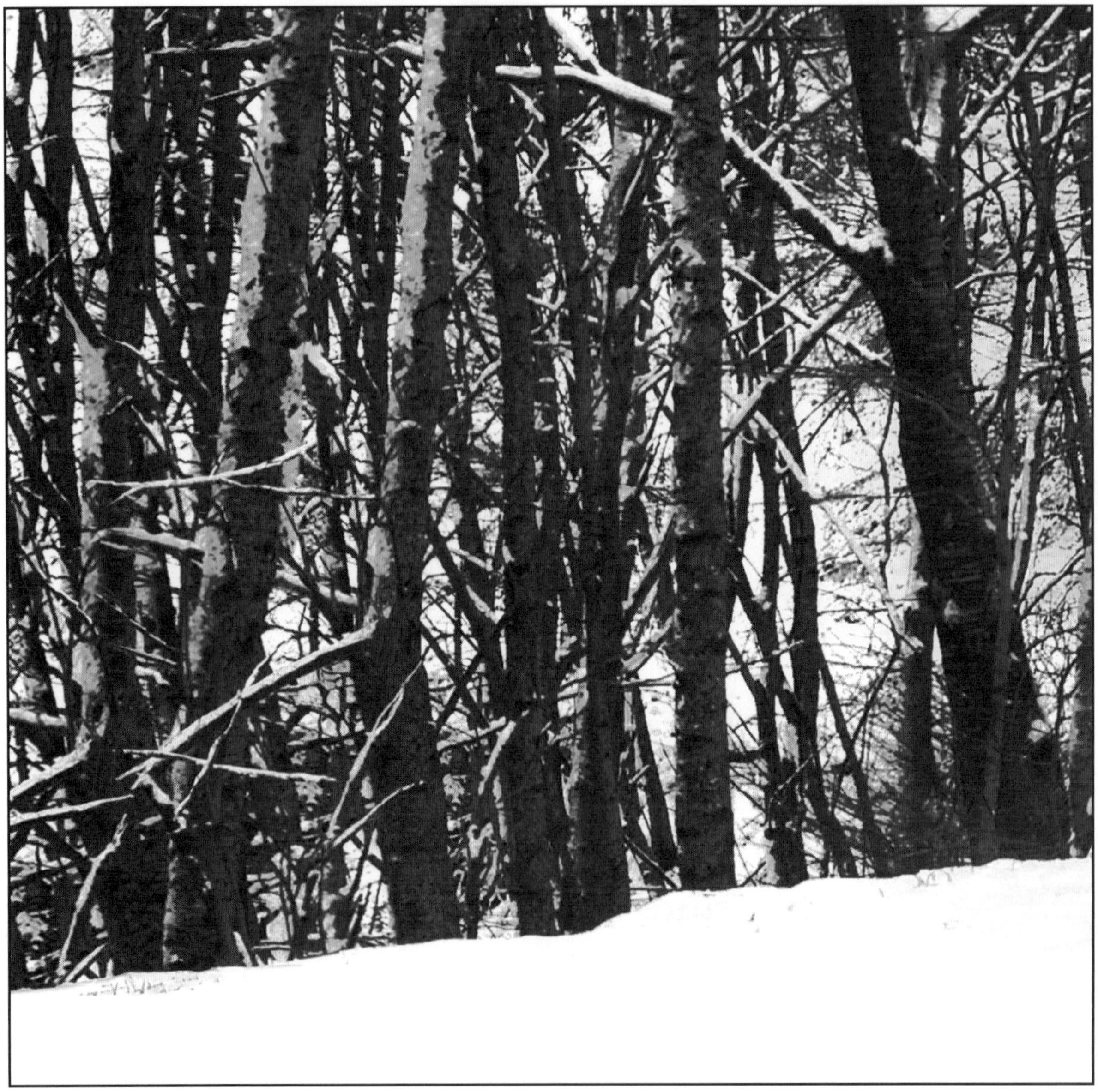

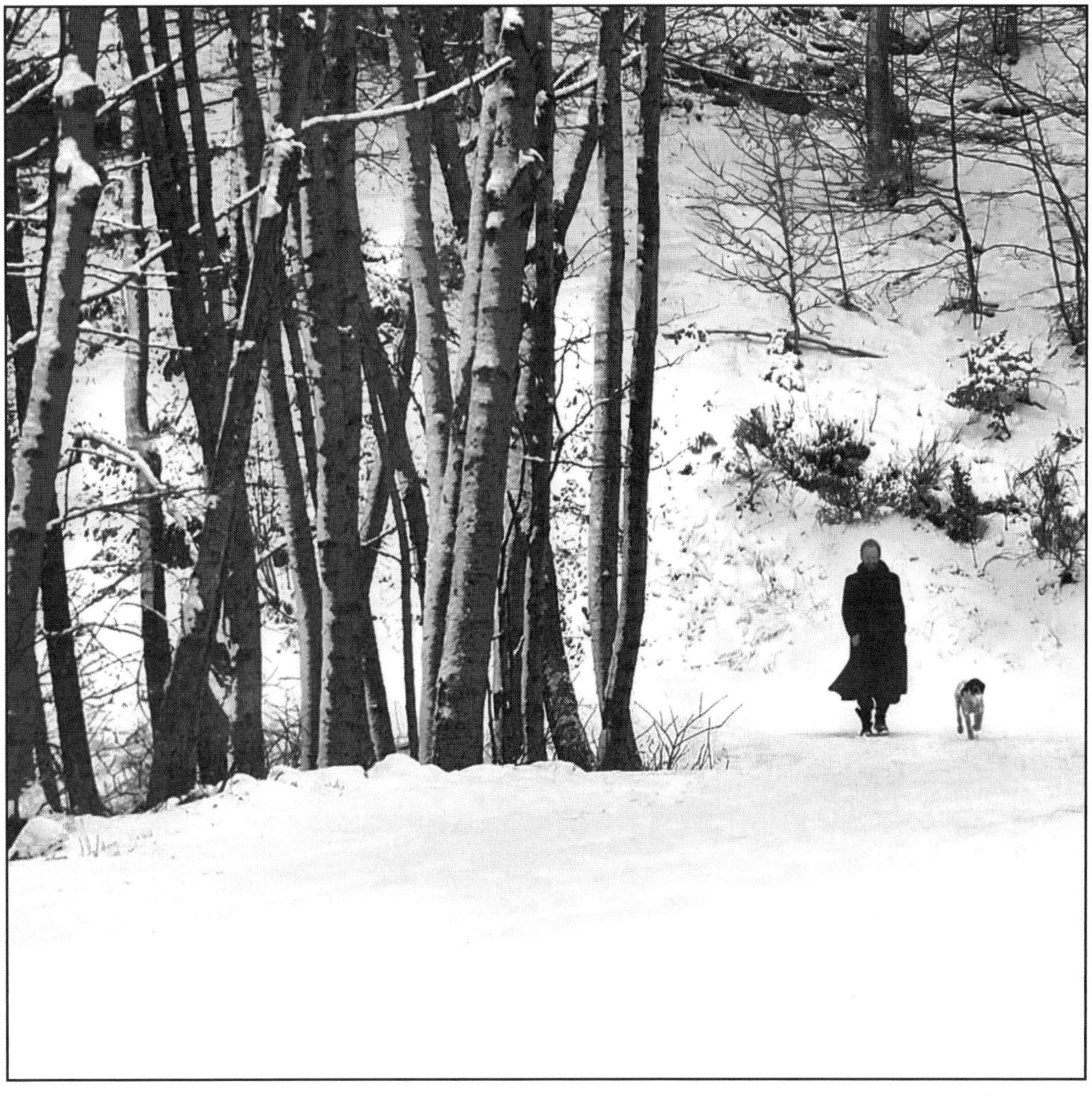

GABRIEL'S MESSAGE

Traditional
Arranged by Sting and Robert Sadin

hail," said he "Thou low-ly mai-den Mar - y." ___ Most high-ly fa-voured la - dy, Glo - - ri - a! (Glo...)___ 2."For known a bles-sed moth-er thou shalt be,___ all gen-er-a-tions laud and ho-nour thee.___ Thy Son shall be E-ma-nu-el, by seers fore-told,___ most high-ly fa-voured la - dy," Glo - - - ri - a!

(Glo...)

3. Then

Gm
B♭add9/D
E♭6
gen - tle Mar - y meek - ly bowed her head. "To me be as it plea - seth
E♭maj7
Cm7
E♭maj7
F
God," she said, "My soul shall laud and mag - ni - fy his ho - ly name." Most
E♭6
Cm7
B♭
high - ly fa - voured la - dy, Glo - - ri - a!
Fadd9/A
E♭6♭5
Gsus4
G
Gm
(Glo…)

SOUL CAKE

Music and Lyrics by Paul Stookey, Tracey Batteast
and Elena Mezzetti

♩ = 120

A soul cake, a soul cake, please good mis-sus a soul cake. An ap-ple, a pear, a plum, or a cher-ry, an-y good thing to make us all

© Copyright 1963 Neworld Media Music Publishers administered by WB Music Corp, USA.
Warner/Chappell North America Limited, London W6 8BS.
Reproduced by permission of Faber Music Ltd.
All Rights Reserved. International Copyright Secured.

merry. A soul cake, a soul cake, please good mis-sus a soul cake. One for Pe-ter, two for Paul and three for him that made us all. (A soul cake, a soul cake, please good mis-sus a soul cake. An ap-ple, a pear, a plum, or a cher-ry, an-y good thing to make us all mer-ry.) 1. God bless the master of this house, and the mistress al-so and all the little children that round your table grow. The cattle in your stable, the dogs at your front door and all that dwell with-in your gates we'll wish you ten times more.

A soul cake, a soul cake, please good mis-sus a soul cake. An ap-ple, a pear, a plum, or a cher-ry, an-y good thing to make us all mer-ry. A soul cake, a soul cake, please good mis-sus a soul cake. One for Pe-ter, two for Paul and three for him that made us all.

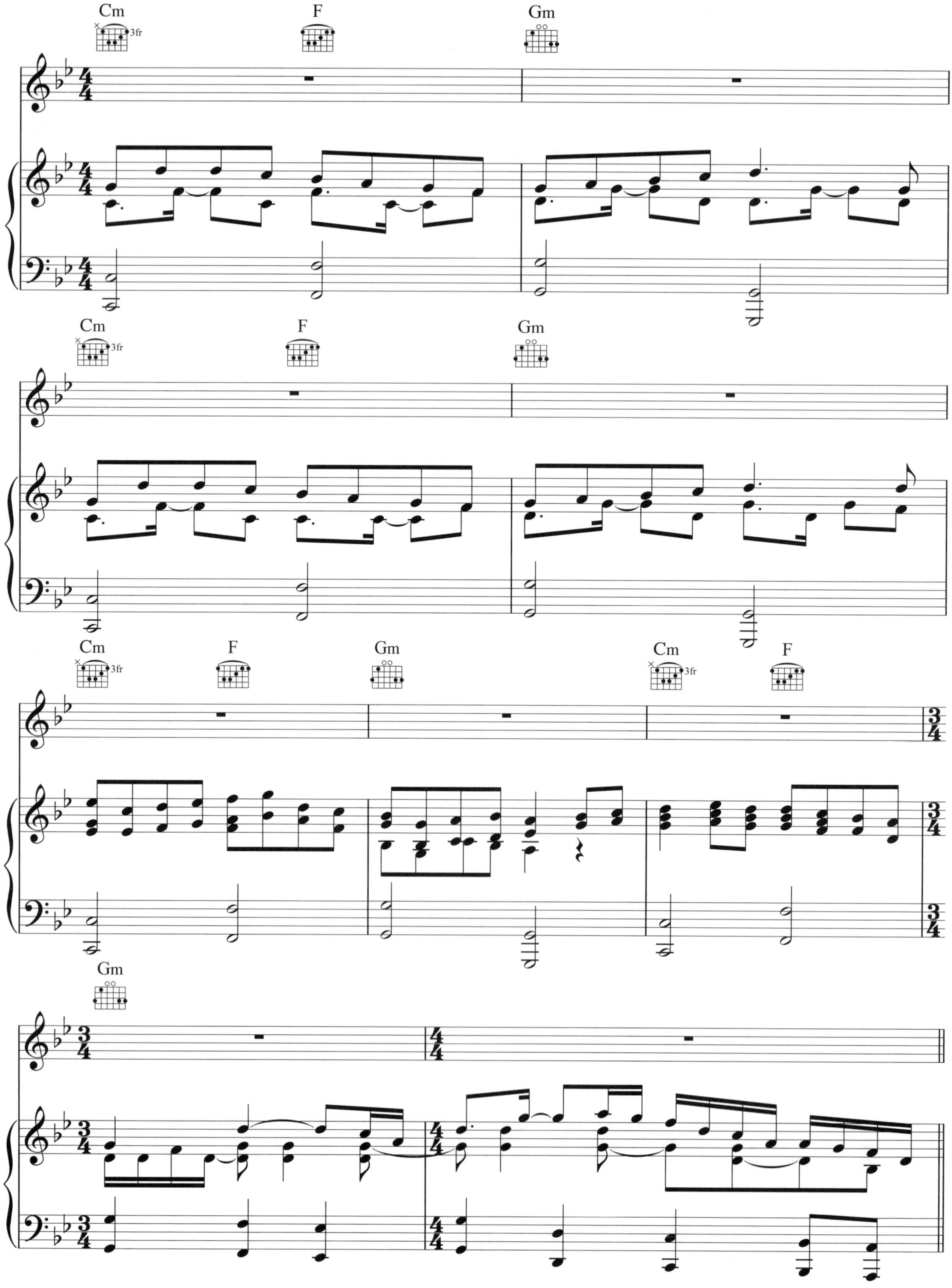
Cm
3fr
F
Gm
Cm
3fr
F
Gm
Cm
3fr
F
Gm
Cm
3fr
F
Gm

2. Go down in-to the cel-lar and see what you can find,
3. The streets are ver-y dir-ty, me shoes are ver-y thin,

if the bar-rels are not emp-ty we'll hope that you'll be kind.
I have a lit-tle pock-et to put a pen-ny in.

We'll hope that you'll be kind with your ap-ple and your pear,
If you have-n't got a pen-ny, a ha'-pen-ny will do,

and we'll come no more a-soul-lin' till Christ-mas time next year.
if you have-n't got a ha'-pen-ny then God bless you.

A

soul cake, a soul cake, please good mis-sus a soul cake. An ap-ple, a pear, a plum, or a cher-ry, an-y good thing to make us all mer-ry. A soul cake, a soul cake, please good mis-sus a soul cake. One for Pe-ter, two for Paul,

1.
three for him that made us all.

2. three for him that made us all.

THERE IS NO ROSE OF SUCH VIRTUE

Traditional
Arranged by Sting and Robert Sadin

♩ = 120

is no rose_____ of such_____ vir - tue_____ as

is the rose_____ that___ bare___ Je - su_____ {There
By

is no rose of such vir- - tue as that
that rose we may well see that

is the rose that bare Je- su.
he is God in per- sons three.

For

in__ this__ rose con-tained it was__ heav-en__ and__ earth__ in lit-tle space. Al - - le - -lu - ia. Al - le - lu - - -

D.S. al Coda   ⊕ *Coda*

-ia. _____ There Al - le - -lu - ia. Al - le - lu - - - - -ia. _____ There is no rose ____ of such ____ vir - tue _____ as is the rose___ that__ bare___ Je - su.___ The an - gels sung - en the___ shep - herds to: Glo - ri - a__ in__ ex - cel - sis de - o. Al - - le - lu - ia. Al - le -

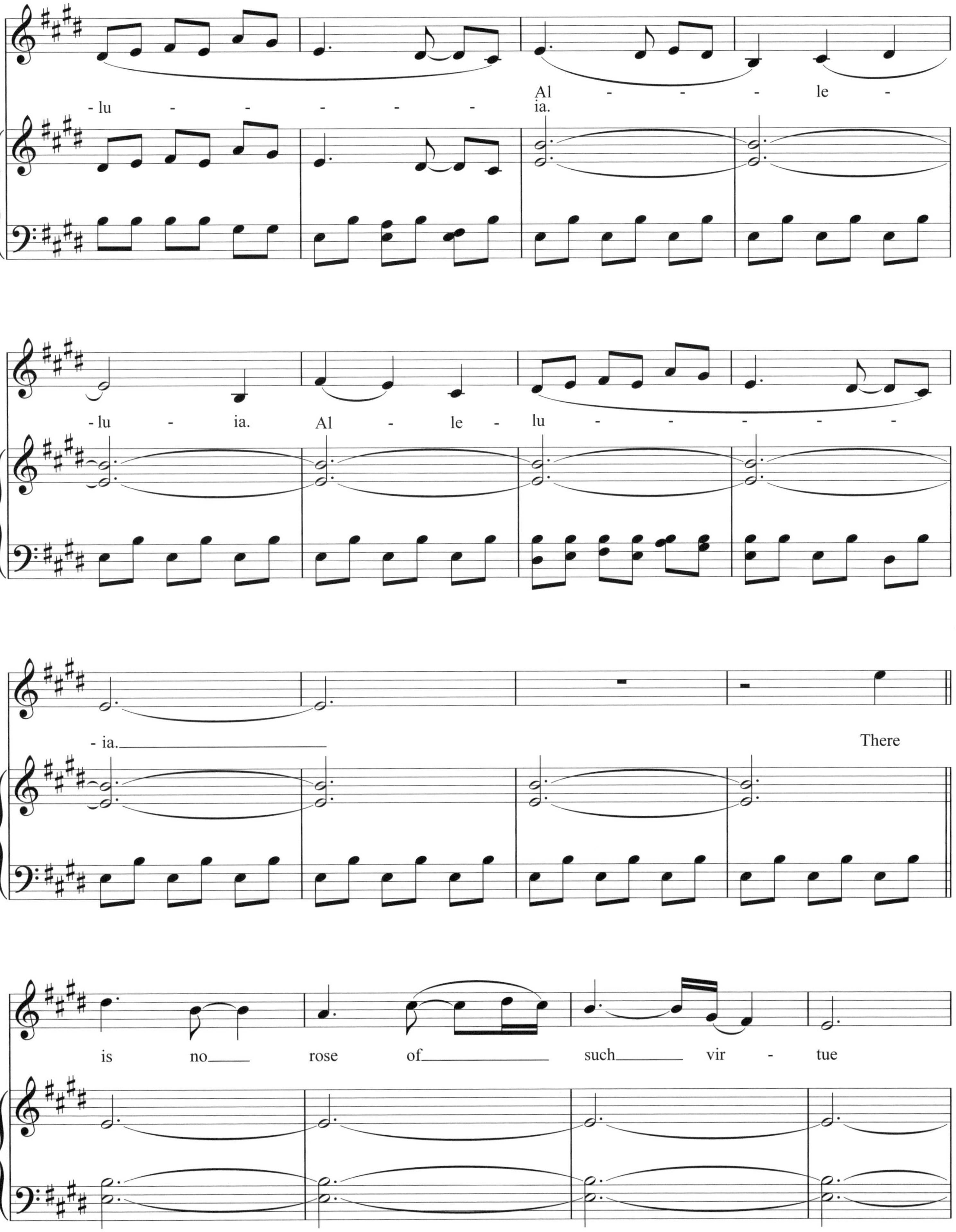
-lu - - - - - ia.
Al - - - le -
-lu - ia. Al - le - lu - - - - - -
- ia.
There
is no rose of such vir - tue

as is the rose that bare Je - su. Al - - - le - lu - ia. Al - le - lu - - - - - - ia.

THE SNOW IT MELTS THE SOONEST

Traditional
Arranged by Sting and Robert Sadin

1. Oh, the snow it melts the soonest when the winds begin to sing. And the corn it ripens fastest when the frost is settling in. And when a woman tells me my face she'll soon forget, be-

(4.) never say me farewell here, no farewell I'll receive. And you shall set me to the stile and kiss and take your leave. I'll stay here until the curlew calls and the martlet takes his wing, oh, the

C5
Csus4
E♭add9
Gm7/D
C5
Fine
3fr
-fore we'll part, I'll wage a croon, she's fain to fol - low - 't yet. 2. Oh, the
snow it melts the soon - est, when the winds be - gins to sing.
A♭6
G7sus4/C
C5
snow it melts the soon - est when the wind be - gins to sing. And the
(3.) snow it melts the soon - est when the wind be - gins to sing. And the
Fadd2
E♭6/9
swal - low skims with - out a thought as long as it is spring. But when spring goes, and win - ter blows, my
bee that flew when sum - mer shone, in win - ter can - not sting. I've seen a wom - an's an - ger melt be-
Fadd2
E♭add9/G
C5
Fm/A♭
1.
A♭maj13
Gm7
C5
lass - ie you'll be fain, for all your pride, to fol - low me, a - cross the stor - my main. 3. Oh, the
- twixt the night and morn, oh, it's sure - ly not a har - der thing to

tame a wom-an's scorn.

Oh...

(Vocal ad lib.)

Gm7/C
A♭maj9
B♭add9/D
Cmadd4
Gm7/C
A♭maj9
B♭add9/D
Cmadd4
Gm7/C
A♭maj9
B♭add9/D
D.S. al Fine
4. Oh,

CHRISTMAS AT SEA

Words by Robert Louis Stevenson
Music by Sting & Mary McMaster

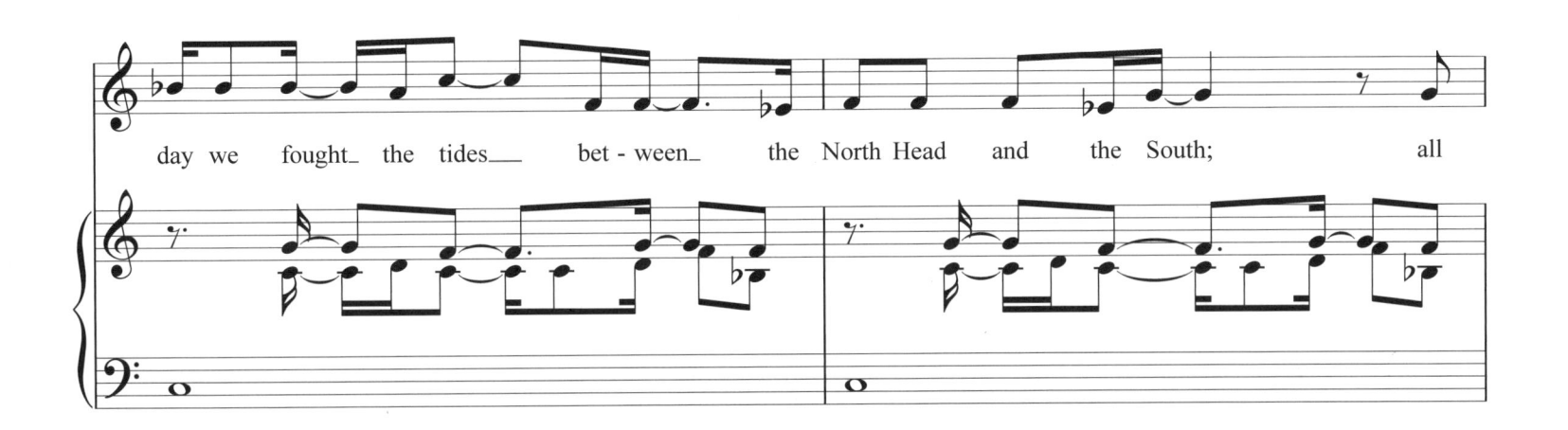

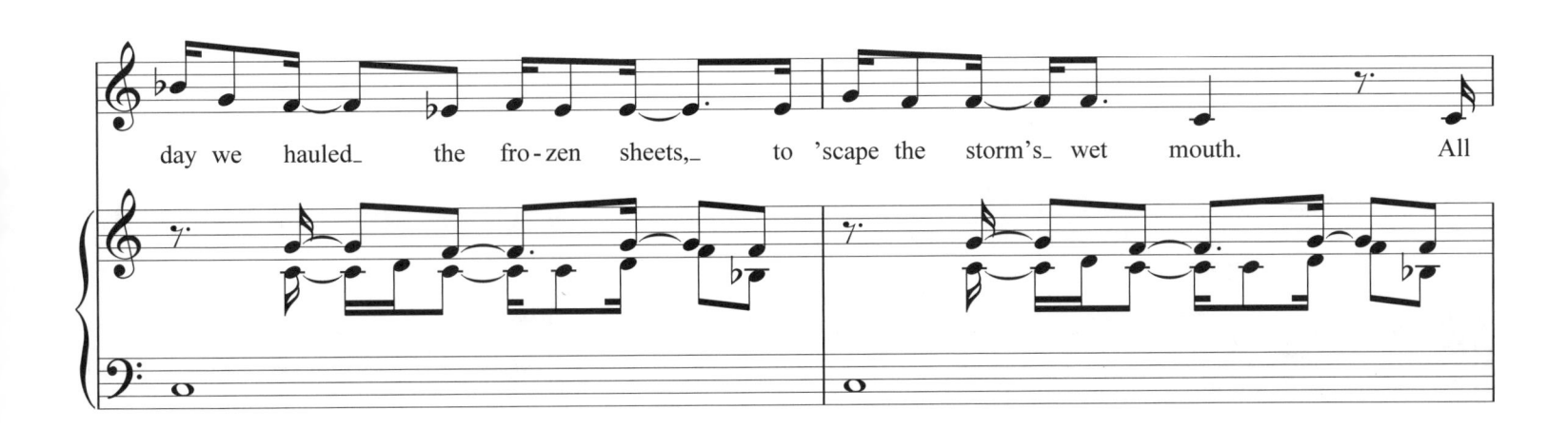

day as cold as char-i-ty, in bit-ter pain and dread, for ver-y life and na-ture we tacked from head to head.

Tho-gra-inn bhith dol dha-chaidh, e ho ro, e ho ro.

Ceud so-raidh bhuam mar bu dual dhomh, e ho hi ri ill iu

o. Ill iu___ o tho-grainn fal-bh.

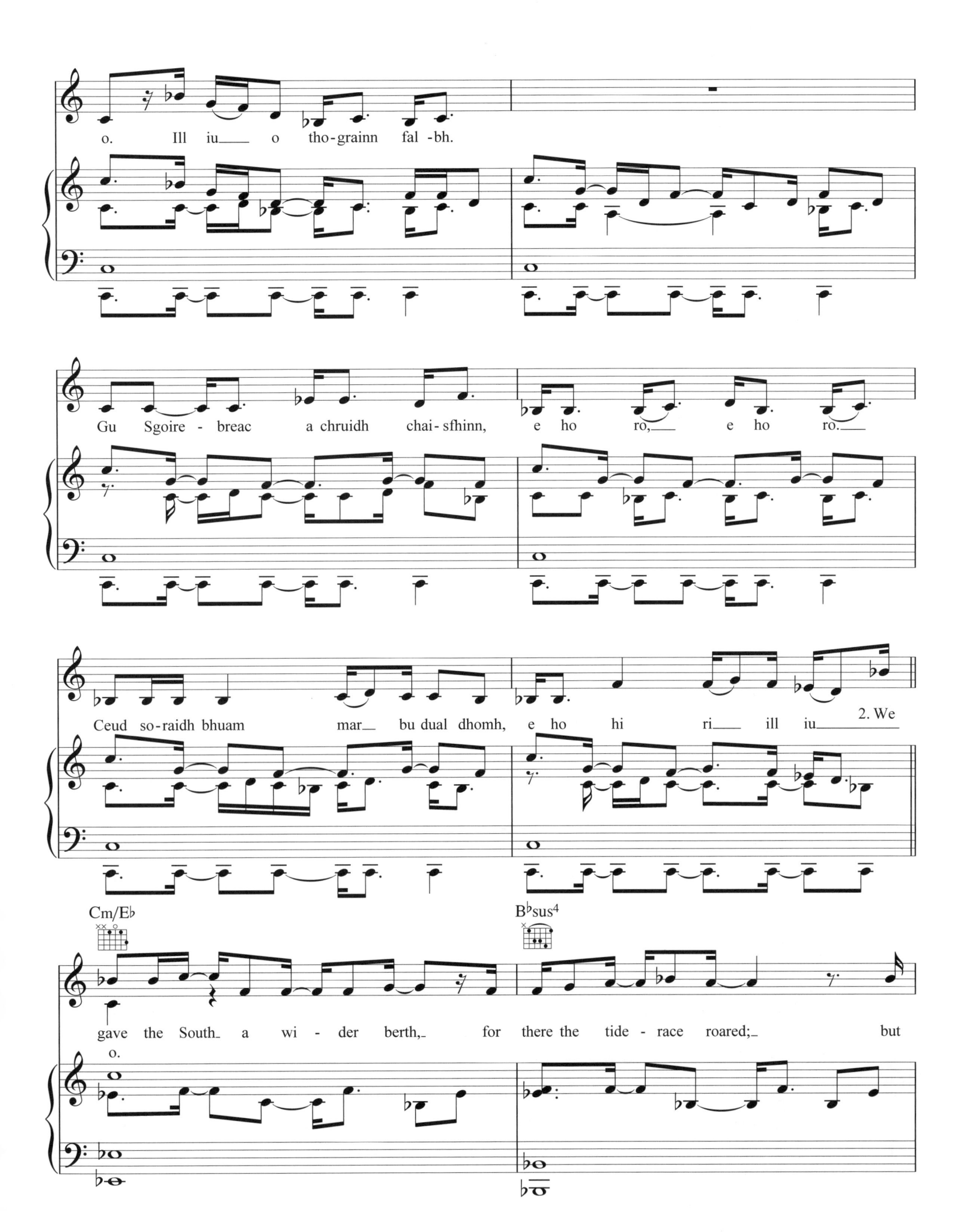

Gu Sgoire - breac a chruidh chai- sfhinn, e ho ro,___ e ho ro.___

Ceud so-raidh bhuam mar___ bu dual dhomh, e ho hi ri___ ill iu___ 2. We

[Cm/E♭] [B♭sus4]

gave the South a wi-der berth,___ for there the tide-race roared;___ but

31

ev-'ry tack we made we brought the North Head close a-board. We saw the cliffs and hou-ses and the brea-kers run-ning high, and the coast-guard in his gar-den, with his glass a-gainst his eye. Tho-grainn bhith dol dha-chaidh, e ho ro, e ho ro.

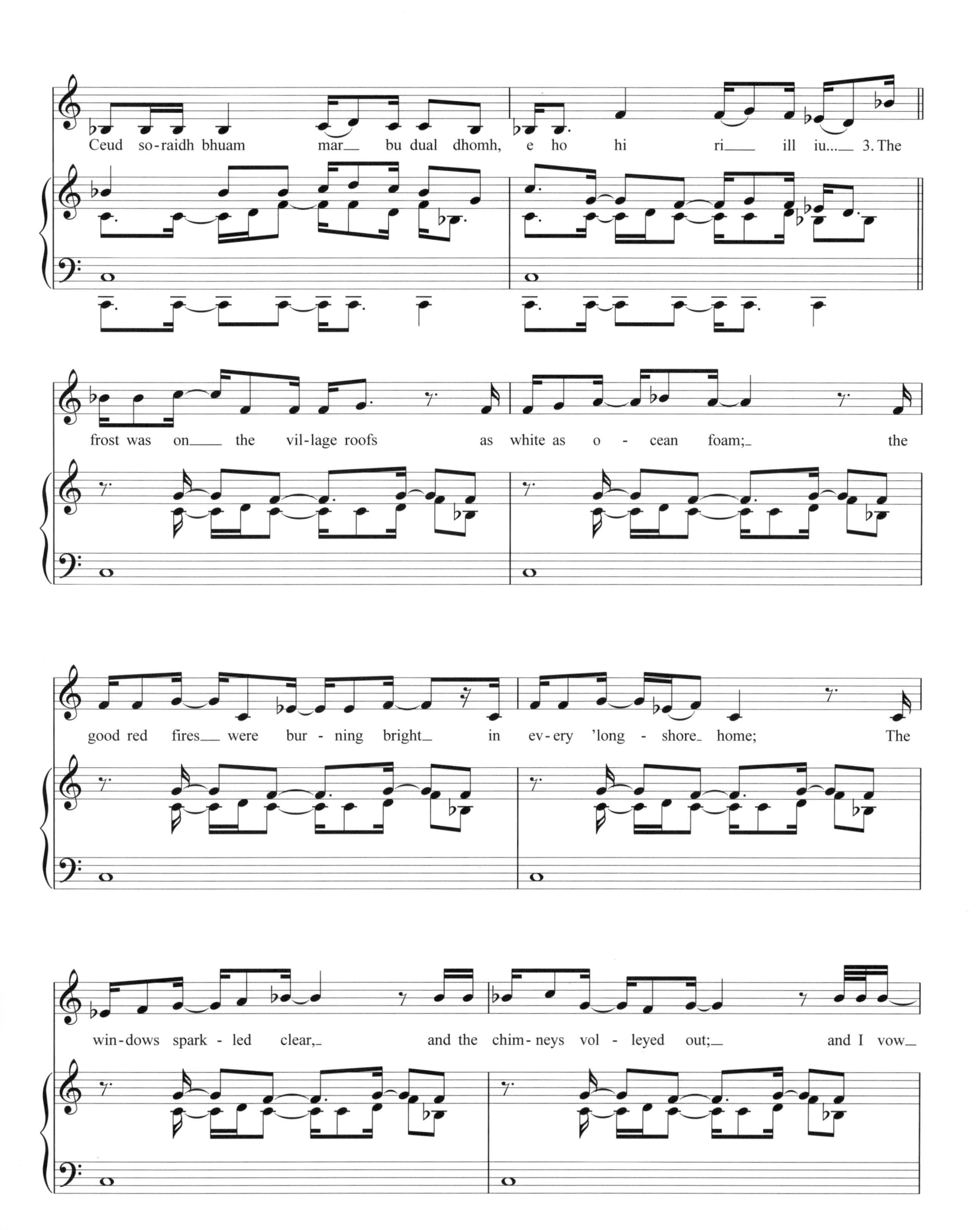

Ceud so-raidh bhuam mar bu dual dhomh, e ho hi ri____ ill iu....___ 3. The frost was on___ the vil-lage roofs as white as o-cean foam;__ the good red fires___ were bur-ning bright___ in ev-ery 'long-shore___ home; The win-dows spark-led clear,___ and the chim-neys vol-leyed out;___ and I vow___

_____ we sniffed_ the vic-tuals as the ves-sel went_ a-bout._

Gu Sgoire - breac a chruidh chai-sfhinn, e ho ro,___ e ho ro.___

Ceud so-raidh bhuam mar_ bu dual dhomh, e ho hi ri___ ill iu___ o.

4. The bells up-on_ the church were rung with a migh-ty jo-vial cheer;_ for it's

E♭

B♭

just that I___ should tell_ you how,_ of all days in the year,_ this day of our_ ad-ver-si-ty__ was bles-sed Christ-mas morn,_ and the house a-bove_ the coast-guard's was the house where I__ was born.____

Tho - grainn bhith dol dha-chaidh, e ho ro,__ e ho ro.__

Gu Sgoire - breac a' chruidh chais- fhionn, e ho hi ri ill iu
o. Ill iu o tho-grainn fal- bh. Gu Sgoire-breac a chruidh chai- sfhinn,
e ho ro, e ho ro. Ceud so-raidh bhuam mar bu dual dhomh,
(Fine)
e ho hi ri ill iu o. Ill iu o tho-grainn fal - bh. 5. And

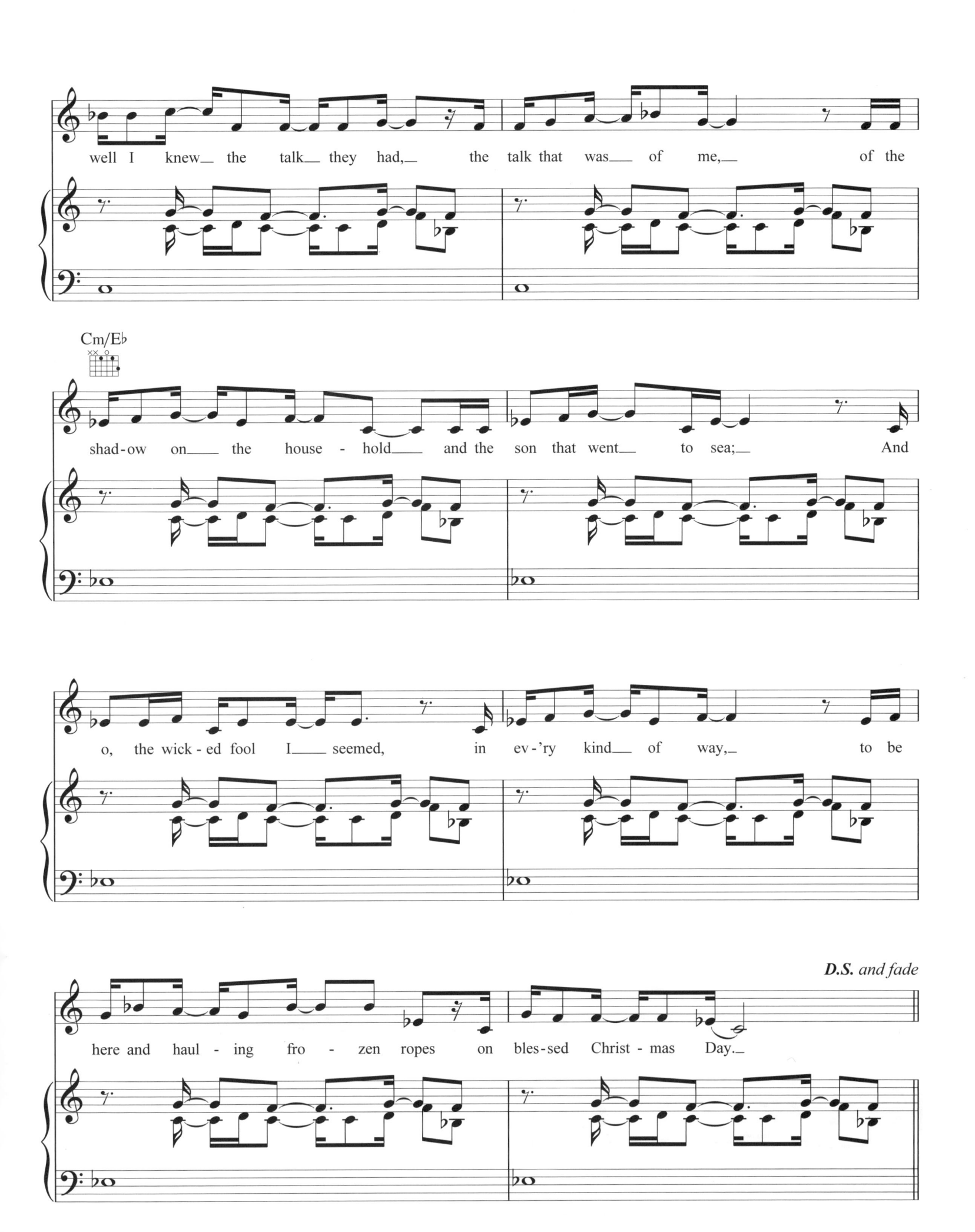

well I knew the talk they had, the talk that was of me, of the

Cm/E♭

shad-ow on the house-hold and the son that went to sea; And

o, the wick-ed fool I seemed, in ev-'ry kind of way, to be

D.S. and fade

here and haul-ing fro-zen ropes on bles-sed Christ-mas Day.

LO, HOW A ROSE E'RE BLOOMING

Music by Michael Praetorius
English Translation by Theodore Baker
Arranged by Sting and Robert Sadin

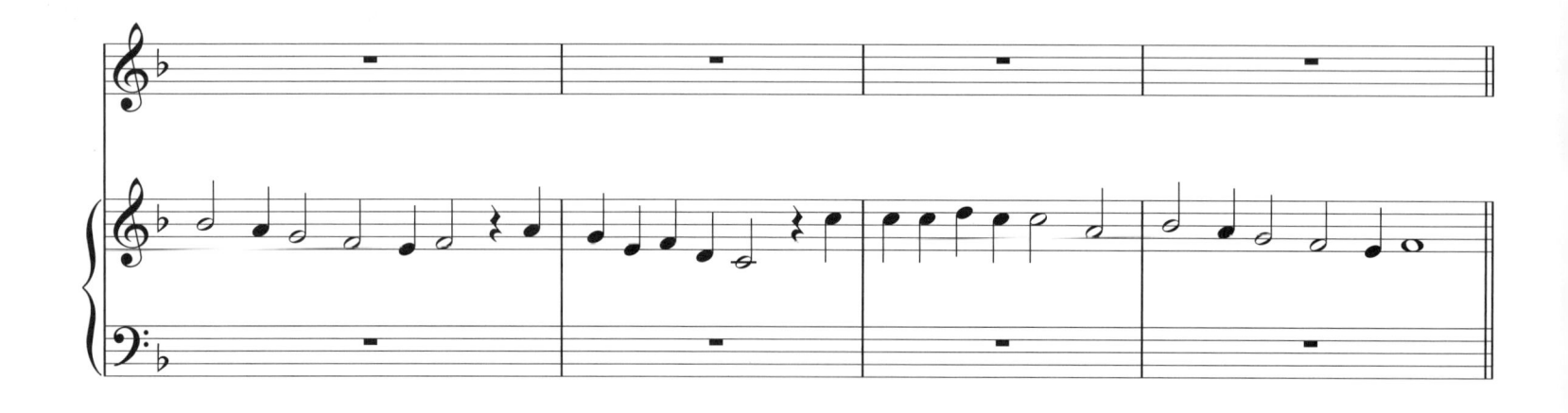

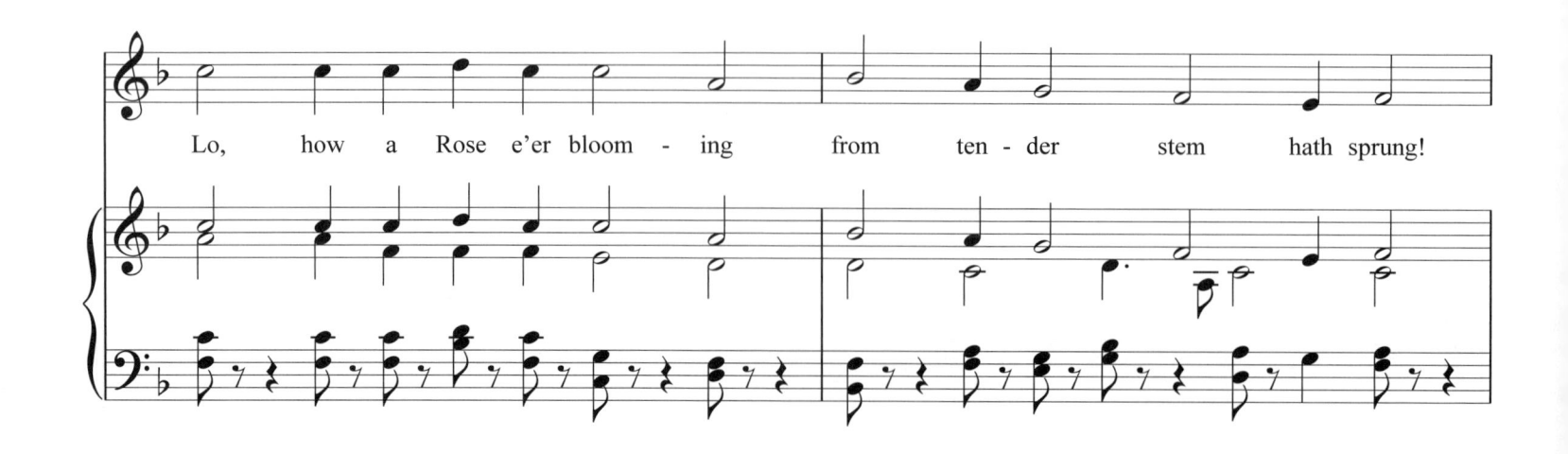

Lo, how a Rose e'er bloom-ing from ten-der stem hath sprung!

© Copyright 2009 Steerpike Limited/Steerpike (Overseas) Limited/EMI Music Publishing Limited.
All Rights Reserved. International Copyright Secured.

Of Jesse's lineage coming, as men of old have sung. It came, a flow'ret bright, amid the cold of winter, when half-spent was the night.

Spoken: Isaiah 'twas fore-told it, the Rose I have in mind. And with Mary we behold it, the Virgin Mother so sweet so kind... (...und hat ein Blüm-lein 'bracht.) She bore to men a Sa-viour, when half spent was the night.

To show God's love a-right, she bore to men a Saviour, when half spent was the night.

COLD SONG

Words by John Dryden
Music by Henry Purcell
Arranged by Sting and Robert Sadin

Lyrics: What pow-er art thou who from be-

-low hast made me rise, un - wil - ling - ly and slow, from beds of ev - er - last - - - ing snow?_____ See'st thou not___ how stiff, how stiff___ and won - drous

(sheet music)

Cm D Edim
breath. Let me, let me, let me,
D♭/F G7/F C/E Cm/E♭ B♭/D
freeze a - gain, let me, let me, freeze
A♭/C G/B B♭ A♭ A♭6♭5 G D7/F♯
a - gain to death. Let me, let me, let me freeze a -
Gsus4 G Cm A♭7/F♯ G Cm
- gain to death.

THE BURNING BABE

Words by Chris Wood & Robert Southwell
Music by Chris Wood

was with sud - den heat which made my heart to glow; and lif - ting
fire, and sighs the smoke, the ash - es shame and scorns; the fuel

up a fear - ful eye to view what fire was near, a pret - ty
jus - tice lay - eth on, and mer - cy blows the coals, the met - al

babe all burn - ing bright did in the air ap - pear.
in this fur - nace wrought are men's de - fil - èd souls.

2. Who, scorch - èd with ex - ces - sive heat, such floods of
4. For which, as now on fire I am to work them

tears__ did shed, as though his floods should quench his
to__ their good, so will I melt in - to a

flames which with his tears__ were fed. A - las, quoth
bath to wash them in__ my blood. With this he

he, but new - ly born in fie - ry heats__ I fry, yet none ap -
van - ished out of sight and swift - ly shrunk_ a - way, and straight I

To Coda ⊕

-proach to warm their hearts or feel my fire__ but I!
call - èd un - to mind that it was

48

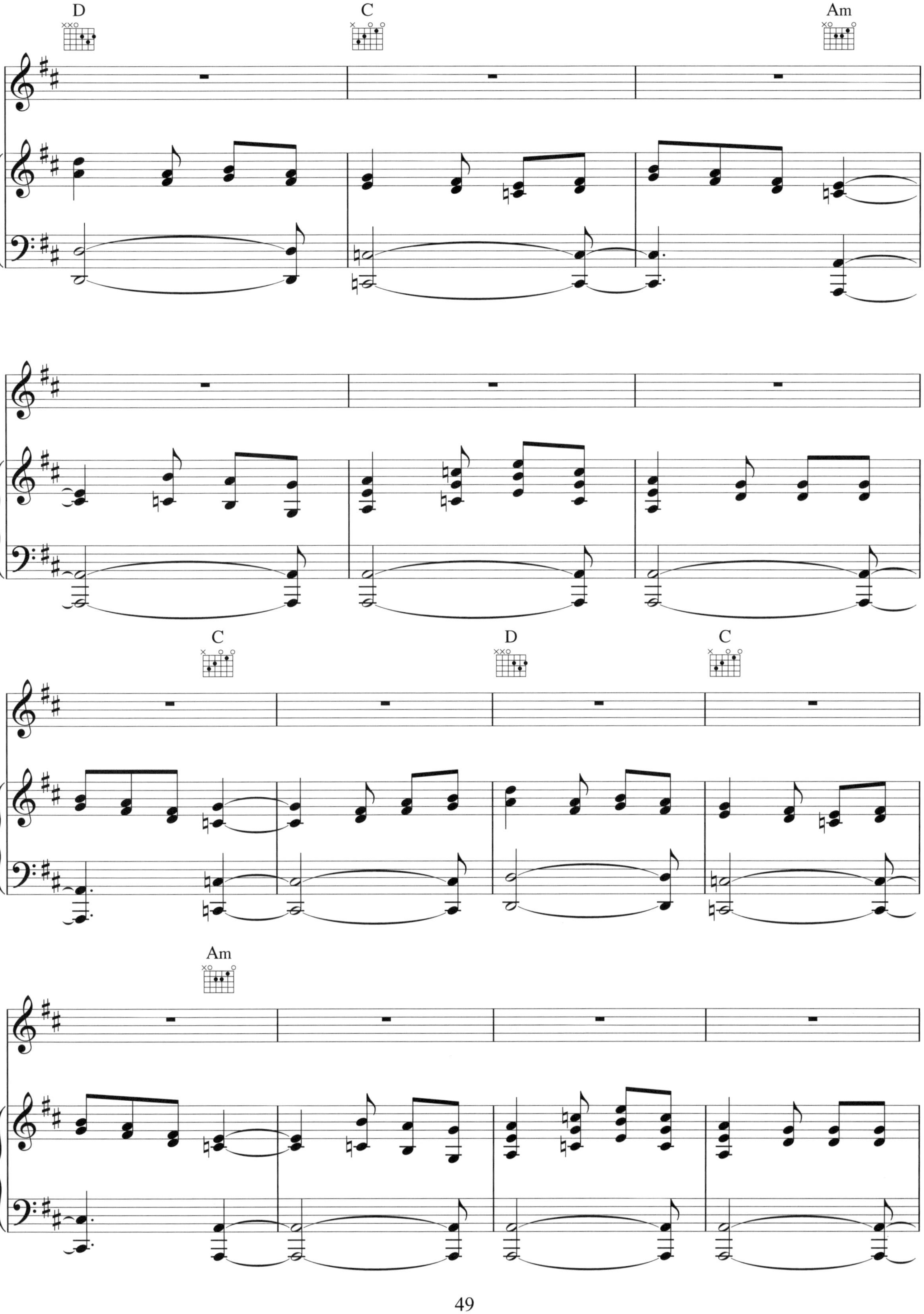
D
C
Am
C
D
C
Am

D.S. al Coda

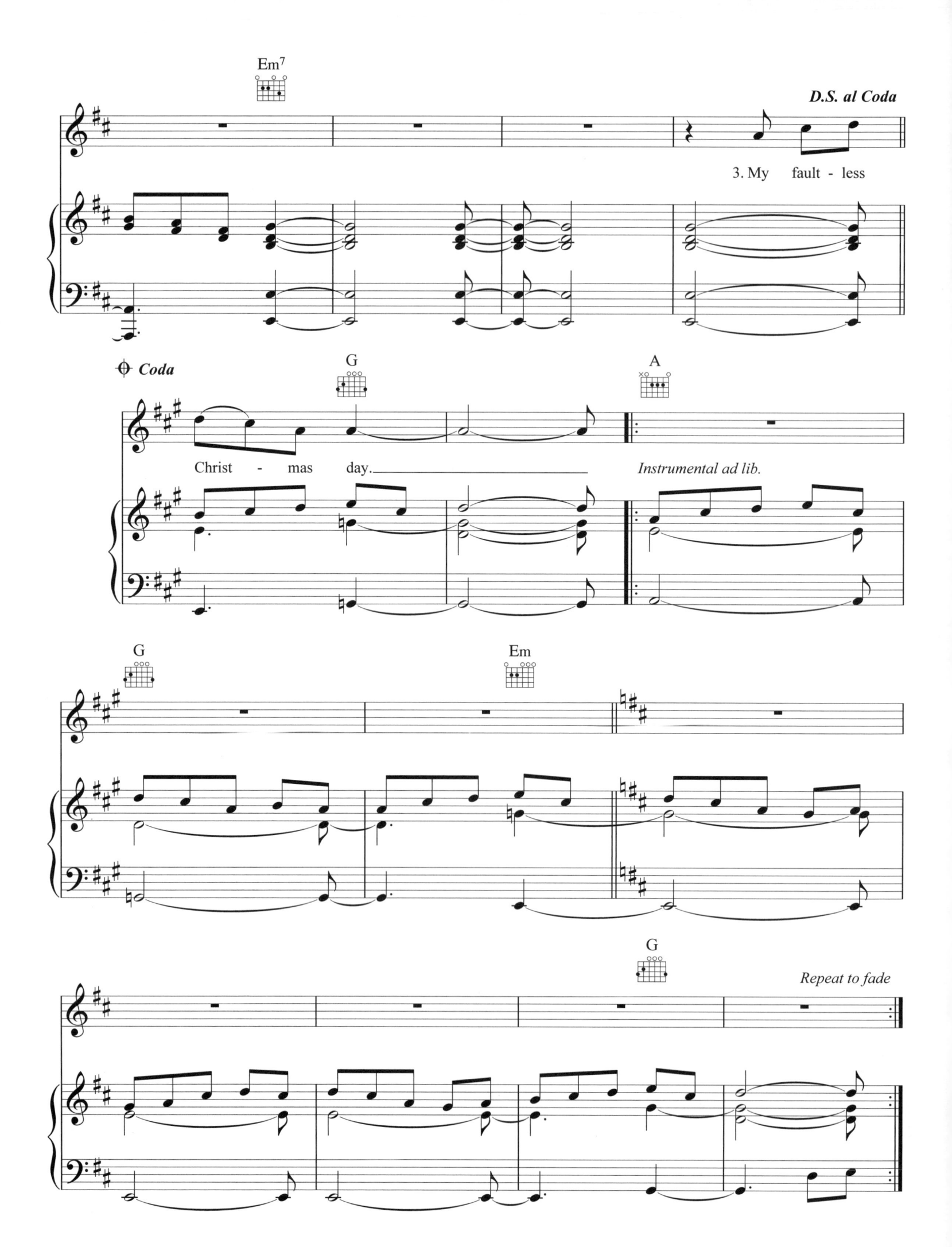

3. My fault-less

Coda

Christ-mas day._____ *Instrumental ad lib.*

Repeat to fade

NOW WINTER COMES SLOWLY

Words by Thomas Betterton
Music by Henry Purcell
Arranged by Sting and Robert Sadin

Original key D♭ major
♩ = 85

Fine

Now

win - ter comes Slow - ly, Pale, Mea - ger and Old. First trem - bling with Age, and then quiv - - - 'ring with Cold. Be -

-numb'd with hard Frost and with Snow cov - 'red o'er, be -
-numb'd with hard Frost and with Snow cov - 'red o'er.
Prays the Sun to Re - store him, prays the Sun to Re -
D.C. al Fine
-store him and Sings as be - fore.

THE HOUNDS OF WINTER

Words & Music by Sting

1. Mer-cu-ry fal-ling, I rise from my bed,
(2.) my coat around my ears,

collect my thoughts together.
I look for my companion.

I have to hold my head.
I have to dry my tears.

It seems that she's gone
It seems that she's gone
3. A season for joy,

and somehow I am pinned
leaving me too soon.
a season for sorrow. Where she's gone, I will surely, surely follow.

by the Hounds
I'm as dark

1.
2, 3.
G Em G Em
D5 Em D5 Em G Em
D5 Em D5 Em
of Win - ter as De - cem - ber She bright - ened my day,
I'm as cold, she
how - ling in the wind.
2. I walk through the day,
I'm as cold, warmed the cold - est night.
But the Hounds of Win - ter,
I'm as cold, as the man in the moon.
they got me in their sights.

I still see her face as beau-ti-ful as day.

It's ea-sy to re-mem-ber, re-mem-ber my love that way.

All I hear is that lone-some, lone-some sound. And the Hounds of Win-ter, they fol-low me down.

To Coda ⊕

I can't make up the fire the way that she could. I spend all my days in the search for dry wood. Board all the windows and close the front door, I can't believe she won't be here anymore. I still see her face as beautiful as day. It's easy to remember,

re-mem-ber my love that way. All I hear is that lone-some, lone-some sound. And the Hounds of Win-ter, they fol-low me down.

D.S. al Coda

Doo, do, do, do, do, doo...

Repeat to fade

Vocal and instrumental ad lib.

BALULALOW

Traditional Words
Music by Peter Warlock
Arranged by Sting and Robert Sadin

© Copyright 2009 Steerpike Limited/Steerpike (Overseas) Limited/EMI Music Publishing Limited.
All Rights Reserved. International Copyright Secured.

my deare hert, young Jesus sweit, pre-pair thy creddil in my spreit. And I sall rock thee in my hert and never mair from thee depart. Ooh,

Ooh, _____ Ooh, ___

2. But I sall praise thee ev-er-more with san-gis sweit un-to thy gloir. The knees of my hert

sall I bow and sing that richt Ba - lu - la - low. Ooh, ooh, ooh.

E♭m7/B♭ E♭/B♭ E♭m7/B♭ E♭/B♭
Ooh, ooh,
E♭m7/B♭ B♭7sus4 E♭/B♭ A♭6/B♭
D.S. al Coda
ooh. And
Coda
E♭m7 E♭ E♭m7 E♭
-low. Ooh, ooh,
E♭m7/A♭ A♭6 E♭
ooh.

CHERRY TREE CAROL

Traditional
Arranged by Sting and Robert Sadin

♩ = 120

Freely

1. When Joseph was an old man, an old man was he, he courted Virgin Mary, the Queen of Galilee. He

(2.) Joseph and Mary were walking one day, here is apples and cherries, so fair to behold. Here is

(Verses 3-7. see block lyrics)

© Copyright 1964, 1971 Geordie Music Publishing Co.
Reproduced by kind permission of Carlin Music Corp., London NW1 8BD.
All Rights Reserved. International Copyright Secured.

courted Virgin Mary, the Queen of Galilee.
apples and cherries, so fair to behold.

1, 2, 4, 5, 6.

2. When

3.

4. Then

7.

Verse 3:
Then Mary spoke to Joseph, so meek and so mild
"Joseph, gather me some cherries for I am with child"
"Oh, Joseph, gather me some cherries for I am with child."

Verse 4:
Then Joseph flew in anger, in anger he flew
"Oh, let the father of the baby gather cherries for you!"
"Oh, let the father of the baby gather cherries for you!"

Verse 5:
So the cherry tree bowed low down, low down to the ground
And Mary gathered cherries while Joseph stood down
And Mary gathered cherries while Joseph stood down.

Verse 6:
Then Joseph took Mary all on his right knee
Crying "Lord, have mercy for what I have done!"
Crying "Lord, have mercy for what I have done!"

Verse 7:
When Joseph was an old man, an old man was he
He courted Virgin Mary, the Queen of Galilee
He courted Virgin Mary, the Queen of Galilee.

LULLABY FOR AN ANXIOUS CHILD

Words & Music by Sting & Dominic Miller

Hush child, let your mom-my sleep

© Copyright 2009 Steerpike Limited/Steerpike (Overseas) Limited/EMI Music Publishing Limited.
All Rights Reserved. International Copyright Secured.

_____ in - to _____ the night _____ un - til _____ we rise. _____ Hush child, let _____ me soothe _ the shin-

-ing tears _ that gath - er in _____ your eyes. _____

Hush child, I _____ won't leave, _ I'll stay _ with you _ to cross _ this Bridge _ of Sighs. _

_____ Hush child, I _____ can't help _ the look _ of ac - cu - sa - tion in _____ your eyes, _

in your eyes. The world is broken now, all in sor - row, wise men hang their heads. Hush child, let your mom - my sleep in - to the night un - til we rise. Hush child, all the strength I'll need

B/D♯ Em C B C♯m7 Aadd9 B
to fight, I'll find in - side your eyes, in your eyes.
Em F♯dim G B/D♯ Em C B
Em F♯dim G B/D♯ Em C B
Em/G Am Am/G D/F♯ D
The world is bro - ken now, all in sor-

- - row, wise men hang their heads.

Hush child, let your mom-my sleep in-to the night un-til we rise.

Hush child, all the strength I need to fight, I'll find with-in your eyes,

in your eyes.

HURDY-GURDY MAN

Words by Wilhelm Müller
Music by Franz Schubert
English Adaptation by Sting
Arranged by Sting and Robert Sadin

plays as best he can. Bare-foot on the ice, he

shuf-fles to and fro and his emp-ty plate, it

on-ly fills with snow. And his emp-ty plate, it

on-ly fills with snow.

No one wants to hear his hur-dy-gur-dy-song,

hun-gry dogs sur-round him and be-fore too long;

he will fall a-sleep and then, be-fore too long,

he'll just let it hap-pen, hap-pen come what may.

Play his hur-dy-gur-dy till his dy-ing day. Watch-ing you, old man, I see my-self in__ you. One day I will play the hur-dy-gur-dy too.__

YOU ONLY CROSS MY MIND IN WINTER

Music by J.S. Bach
Words by Sting
Arranged by Sting and Robert Sadin

Al-ways this win-ter child, De-cem-ber sun sits low a-gainst the sky.

Cold light on fro-zen fields, the cat-tle in their sta-ble low-ing. When

two walked this win-ter road, ten thous-and miles seemed noth-ing to us then. One walks with

© Copyright 2009 Steerpike Limited/Steerpike (Overseas) Limited/EMI Music Publishing Limited.
All Rights Reserved. International Copyright Secured.

heav-y tread, the space be-tween their foot-steps slow - ing.___ All day the snow did fall, what's left of the day is close drawn in. I speak your name___ as if you'd ans-wer me.___ But the si-lence of the snow is deaf-'ning. How well do I re-call our ar-gu-ments. Our lo-gic owed no debts or re-com-pense. Phi

-os - o - phy and faith were ghosts that we would chase un - til the gates of heav-en were bro - ken. But some-thing makes me turn, I don't know, to see an - oth - er's foot-steps there in the snow. I smile to my-self and then I won-der why it is you on - ly cross my mind in win - ter.

Your Guarantee of Quality:

As publishers, we strive to produce every book
to the highest commercial standards.

The music has been freshly engraved and the book has
been carefully designed to minimise awkward page turns
and to make playing from it a real pleasure.

Particular care has been given to specifying
acid-free, neutral-sized paper made from pulps which
have not been elemental chlorine bleached.

This pulp is from farmed sustainable forests and
was produced with special regard for the environment.

Throughout, the printing and binding have
been planned to ensure a sturdy, attractive publication
which should give years of enjoyment.

If your copy fails to meet our high standards,
please inform us and we will gladly replace it.